The Little
Discovery

by Ann Roberts
Illustrations by Martha Hardy

LITTLE BOOKS WITH **BIG** IDEAS

Reprinted 2011
Published 2009 by A&C Black Publishers Limited
36 Soho Square, London W1D 3QY
www.acblack.com

ISBN 978-1-9060-2971-5

Text © Ann Roberts 2008
Series Editor, Sally Featherstone
Illustrations © Martha Hardy, 2006
Cover photographs © Emma Rothery, Jolly Giraffes
Nursery, Leeds and Sarah Featherstone

Printed in Great Britain by Latimer Trend & Company Limited

This book is produced using paper that is made from wood grown in
managed, sustainable forests. It is natural, renewable and recyclable.

The logging and manufacturing processes conform to the environmental
regulations of the country of origin.

**To see our full range of titles
visit www.acblack.com**

Contents

Introduction

A discovery bottle is a vehicle for getting children to respond, experiment, think and talk. According to their construction and contents, discovery bottles can stimulate different senses by making sounds, emitting aromas or presenting small worlds. This book offers practitioners ideas for making discovery bottles from simple plastic containers and using them for work with children in the Early Years Foundation Stage and into Year 1. The interesting contents and presentation of the bottles attract young children to want to explore and use them in their play.

Discovery bottles are inexpensive and easily made. They are suitable for a wide range of ages, from young babies to toddlers and pre-school children, children with additional needs and even some older children. Depending on the contents, they can be used across all the areas of learning and reach all six of the EYFS levels of development.

There are many plastic bottles available in a wide variety of shapes and sizes. You should be able to collect quickly and easily all those you need for the activities in this book. The instructions are written for adults to make the bottles, and this will certainly be the case with younger children. However, older children will be able to take over some, if not all, of the construction, and all children will be able to help with decisions about the contents. It goes without saying that particular care is needed to ensure that the bottles are thoroughly clean before you start, and that children should not use powerful adhesives. Practitioners working with very young children must be alert to swallowing and choking hazards. Some children may be allergic to various contents suggested for some of the bottles. Be alert to the possibility of allergic reactions and always check with parents. See the guidance on health and safety on page 6.

Making the bottles is important, but so is their storage and care. It is possible to build up a collection that the children can access and use again and again, and which will provide a rich resource for your work.

Discovery bottles need to be made very well so they look attractive and will stimulate play and talk. The size and shape must be appropriate for the age or stage of the child. Young children are very mobile and much of their learning comes from looking, so they will enjoy these colourful and portable objects. The bottles can be rolled to stimulate reaching and grasping or to encourage mobility. Held in the hand, they can be used to promote observation. The contents, design and the practitioner's understanding of child development will all contribute to the way they are used. As children get to the latter part of the Foundation Stage, they can start to develop their own discovery bottles with supervision. They can use their imagination and their skills to produce some very individual bottles of their own.

Beginning a collection is simple, but underpinning this is the understanding of child development and play, and how these apparently simple props can facilitate high quality experiences at home or in an Early Years setting. This book will provide an excellent starting point for developing work with discovery bottles and give you simple, helpful and important information so that you can make the most of them.

Storage, organisation and resource presentation

If you follow most of the activities in this book, you'll be collecting a lot of bottles! The storage of resources is important, as is the presentation to children.

Health and safety is paramount with any Early Years equipment. Using discovery bottles is very rewarding but there are also potential hazards and it is important to be aware of these. For example, bottles can split and leak, small contents can be swallowed and some children may be allergic to various contents suggested.

If you are working in an Early Years setting, you will be operating in line with the Welfare Requirements in the Early Years Foundation Stage (see 'Suitable premises, environment and equipment' on page 33 of EYFS document, May 2008 edition).

Health and safety

▶ The bottles must be clean. They must be washed in hot water, dried and wiped with hygienic wipes. All labels should be removed. Some will soak off. For others, you will need to use a proprietary cleaner (for example, Sticky Stuff Remover). These are solvents and all traces must be removed from the bottles before they are offered to children.

▶ The bottle lids must be checked. Ensure that they are securely fixed, using a waterproof glue, and that the bottle contents can't leak out.

▶ The bottles that are to contain liquid must not be too large or heavy for the children who will use them when they are full. Smaller-sized bottles are more suitable for younger children.

▶ Regular maintenance checks should be part of your daily routine. Some plastic bottles are quite thin and won't last long. Always check them before use to ensure they are whole, watertight and have no jagged or sharp edges. This is particularly important if you are re-using bottles that have been put aside for a time.

The guidance above is not comprehensive. Allowing access and choices for children means ensuring a balance of risk, health and safety. Follow the health and safety policies of your setting and local authority, and carry out a risk assessment before any activity.

Choosing bottles

You'll need several different types of bottle. Small clear ones (the sort sold for juice or water) are ideal for many of the activities in this book. Larger bottles (1.5 to 2 litre) will be needed for others. For some (particularly in Section Five), you'll need the sort of bottles used for sports drinks that have drinking nozzles.

Many of the smaller bottles have the maker's name and other information printed directly onto the plastic. This is difficult to remove and you may want to search for small bottles with labels that can be peeled off. Most of the bottles you'll need are the 'see through' type made of transparent plastic. However, for others, it's important that the contents are not seen, and for these you'll need bottles made of white or coloured plastic. Whenever you can, choose bottles with the widest possible necks. This will make it easier to get the intended contents into the bottle.

The shapes of the bottles are very important. Bottles with smooth sides roll more freely and move more quickly than bottles with ribbed or flat sides. If you hope to promote mobility, such as crawling, smooth-sided bottles are more useful. If it's important that the bottle doesn't move, choose one with flat sides.

Organisation of resources

A lot is said about creating environments that will enable child-initiated learning, so if children are to have choice and initiate their own activities, they need to be able to get at the resources.

Try displaying your collection of discovery bottles in low-level wicker or willow baskets. This allows access and opportunity for babies and younger children to see a range and choose which bottle to play with.

Wine racks are ideal for storing bottles. Placing the bottles in a low wine rack will allow older babies and toddlers to help themselves – they can choose what they want and slide the bottles out independently.

If your setting has a low window ledge, this is an ideal place to display the bottles. The light coming through the windows can highlight the colours and contents. However, be aware that bottles can get hot on a sunny window sill. Not only does this create risks when picked up, but bottles that don't contain liquid have been known to melt!

Bottles make an attractive display, which requires only a small amount of time for maintenance. Coasters and old CDs make good display bases. Crêpe and tissue paper can add colour. Try laying out the bottles on the floor in a large circle. Sit the baby or small child in the centre of the circle so they can move their head and eyes to see the bottles around them.

Suspending the bottles securely from a baby-gym frame or the ceiling is another way to change the child's view and access, as the bottles swing gently in the air.

Themes and collections

Group the bottles into collections. This allows a range of opportunities to explore and discover, and reinforces the idea or concept of the bottles' focus.

Use stickers on the top of the bottle with symbols or colours for a quick visual way of gathering collections together.

Focus collections around the senses – 'smelly' bottles, bottles that make a noise and brightly coloured bottles. Plastic bottles are easily sourced and so can be replaced and renewed easily.

Discovery bottles are ideal for personalisation. Children can have individual bottles decorated with photographs and labelled with their names. These make ideal items for children to take home for special occasions, such as birthdays or seasonal festivals and celebrations.

Where do ideas for collections come from?

There are many possibilities for individual bottles and collections. Use your own knowledge of child development to inform the contents and use of the bottles. Observing the impact on the baby, toddler or older child will help you to consider the appropriate next steps.

Follow the children's interests. If a child is very interested in a specific resource, such as trains or an animal, use this as the basis for creating a bottle. Trends and fashion interests in TV and stories also appeal to children. Check out the recent trends by watching children's programmes or by visiting local bookshops and libraries to keep up to date.

Child-initiated bottles

Let older children experiment with making their own bottles. Bottles are ideal for water play and children will love creating potions or making small world environments. You will need:

▶ a supply of bottles of all sizes and shapes

▶ access to water

▶ food colourings

▶ funnels, pipettes and tubes

▶ brushes to clean the bottles

▶ collections of creative items (pompoms, buttons, pipe cleaners and feathers)

▶ small pocket money toys

▶ glitter, sequins and confetti

▶ small stickers

▶ glue (children could use PVA glue or waterproof tape, but plastic glue should be applied by an adult).

Set up a clean surface. The bottles should be cleaned before giving them to the children, but it's good practice to let them help to clean the bottles first and allow them to dry.

Have paper and pencils ready so that children can plan a design for their bottles and their contents. Some children may start but change their ideas as they try things out. Don't forget, it's the process that is most important.

Once they have made their bottles, they will need to seal them. Put the top on loosely first and check what it looks like. When they are satisfied, you can help them to glue the lids on.

Ask the children to give the bottle a name and add any stickers or any labels they may want. They may want to go on to make more bottles. Some children will be less interested in the finished product and will find using the funnels, pouring and filling more important.

Section One

Starting early with discovery bottles – babies and bottles

This resource will not be found in educational catalogues and so is unique. However, it does build on the natural instinct of babies to reach and grasp. From a very young age, babies grasp at their own milk or water bottles and try to hold them for themselves. The idea of discovery bottles builds on this natural behaviour, stimulating the baby's senses and providing a different kind of nourishment – that of the mind.

Discovery bottles for babies can be introduced into 'tummy time'. Babies spend a lot of time sleeping on their backs and in buggies and car seats. To balance this, they need time lying on their stomachs. In this position they can watch the bottles roll and look inside them. This helps their physical and mental development, and we all know that developing young babies' senses through play has important benefits in stimulating their young minds.

It is essential that bottles are clean and are wiped and checked regularly. It is a reflex action for babies to put their toys in their mouths as they explore with all their senses, and they need to be protected against infection because their immune systems are not fully developed.

Start by collecting a range of small-sized plastic bottles. There are many designs on the market nowadays. You need only to scan the shelves in a large supermarket and you will see an array of sizes and shapes. There will be lots in the area devoted to bottled waters, but you'll also find a variety amongst the juices and dairy products. Choose bottles with the widest necks you can find.

You will need to remove the labels from the bottles and this can be quite difficult. Most can be removed by soaking in soapy water, perhaps overnight. For more stubborn labels you may need a proprietary solvent (for example, Sticky Stuff Remover) but be sure to wash the bottle thoroughly afterwards. Some solvents attack the plastic of some bottles, so watch out!

Use your discretion when choosing, but on the whole it is best to avoid bottles that have contained non-food products. Smaller-sized fruit or water bottles are not too heavy when full for a baby to manage, so seek out suitable sizes and shapes of plastic bottles and begin by creating some of the ideas in this chapter. They are designed to stimulate your senses too and once you grasp the idea of the discovery bottle, you will find that very quickly you will have some new ideas of your own to add to those offered here.

Most of the other items you will need will already be in your setting. As well as the bottles, it will be useful to have plastic tubing, a jug and a funnel. You can easily make a funnel by cutting the base off a plastic bottle (choose one with the narrowest neck you can find). You'll also need glue to stick the lids onto the bottles. We recommend using a waterproof glue or plastic impact glue (such as UHU) for bottles that contain water and for those that may be sucked!

Black and White

The black and white discovery bottle collection

What you need:

▶ six or more small plastic bottles (clean and dried).

▶ collections of black and white objects, for example:
black and white small plastic cows from a farm set
black and white small mathematical plastic cubes
black and white pipe cleaners – twisted around a pencil to make spirals
black and white buttons
black and white pompoms
black and white plastic confetti

▶ water, a small funnel and a small measuring jug

▶ plastic glue such as UHU

▶ antiseptic wipes – for ensuring hygiene (important for all children, particularly babies)

▶ black and white circles for the floor – for presentation.

Reference to EYFS Development Statements

Communication, Language and Literacy: language for thinking, page 49
0–11 months – Look, listen and note: how babies concentrate on or gaze intently at things that catch their interest.

Communication, Language and Literacy: handwriting, page 61
8–20 months – Begin to bring together hand and eye movements to fix on and make contact with objects.

What and why

A baby's eyes will be developing for some time after they are born. The sharp definition between black and white helps visual discrimination and focus.

Before you start

Choose empty bottles that are small enough for a baby to grip. There are some small water bottles with sports lids or 'shooter' tops. These have thinner necks and are easier to grasp. If you put water in the bottle, don't fill it too full or it will be too heavy. A baby's wrist is still developing and will not be able to support a full bottle.

What to do:

1. Collect your bottles. For some of the items you will need bottles with wide necks. Check that none have labels or paper on them. Wash and clean them inside and out. Dry them.
2. Decide whether the bottles will be dry (without water added) or with water. Air in the bottles has one effect, water another. Or, if you can, make 2 sets – one with water and one without.
3. Choose what to put in each bottle. Avoid putting too many different items in one bottle. When you are satisfied that there are enough items in the bottle to stimulate the children, test it by closing the lid and holding it yourself.
4. Test the effect of the materials inside by rolling, tipping and holding the bottles individually – do this before you seal them for good.
5. Apply the PVA glue to the necks of the bottles, screw on the lids, tighten and wait until dry.
6. Babies will put the bottles in their mouths, so have antiseptic wipes to hand and wipe the bottles after every session.

And another idea...

▶ It is important to present new resources in an attractive way. For example, you could put the bottles on black and white coasters made by covering old CDs with sticky-backed plastic. Try putting a trail of black and white circles on the floor with a bottle on each. Let the babies crawl to them and discover and explore.

▶ Place the bottles on a washable soft bath mat (choose black or white) to denote a boundary.

▶ Take the bottles outside in a low wicker basket so babies can explore and use them in the open air.

▶ Make a pure white collection or make a black set of bottles.

▶ Take some black CD cases and insert items that are white – so that babies can explore flat surface images as well as cylinders.

13

All That Glitters

Adding sparkle and shine to baby bottles

What you need:

▶ six or more clean bottles

▶ several different food colourings

▶ glitter (try to find more than one sort)

▶ silver and gold confetti (various designs are available in card shops)

▶ a funnel

▶ a small jug

▶ plastic glue such as UHU.

Reference to EYFS Development Statements

Knowledge and Understanding of the World: designing and making, page 81
0–11 months – Explore objects and materials with hands and mouth.

Communication, Language and Literacy: handwriting, page 61
8–20 months – Begin to bring together hand and eye movements to fix on and make contact with objects.

What and why

Babies like shiny objects and the different coloured glitters will swirl and move, keeping their attention as they look at the bottles. This works particularly well alongside a very strong colour such as red.

Before you start

Collect all the bottles, check they are clean and remove the labels. Use a baby bottlebrush to clean inside them. Collect together all the contents and a funnel or paper cone to help with the transfer into the bottles.

What to do:

1. Select the collection of items to put into the bottles.
For example:
  ▶ red food colouring in water with gold stars
  ▶ no food colouring with silver and gold confetti
  ▶ yellow food colouring with silver stars.
There are many different combinations. Experiment – keeping in mind the need for visual impact.

2. Use a funnel and jug to fill the bottles. Don't fill them too full.

3. Baby oil can be used to create a thickening effect when shaken.

4. When you think that there are enough items in the bottle to stimulate the children, test it by closing the lid and holding it yourself. Roll and tip the bottle to see what happens.

5. When you are satisfied, apply the glue to the necks of the bottles, screw on the lids, tighten and wait until dry.

6. Babies will put the bottles in their mouths, so have antiseptic wipes to hand and wipe the bottles after every session.

And another idea...

▶ Present the bottles on shiny coasters in a line so the babies can choose.

▶ Hang the bottles from a baby-gym frame.

▶ Use plastic ziplock bags – insert shiny objects, add water and hair gel and seal up.

▶ Use shiny pipe cleaners, twisted and inserted in a bottle.

▶ Put Christmas tinsel or tinsel pompoms in the bottles to create a shiny effect.

Squeeze and Smell

Sensory bottles for babies

What you need:

I will need

▶ six or more small, clean bottles. The best are the 'Fruit Shoot' style of bottle that has a sports cap with a pop-up drinking nozzle

▶ a collection of items with powerful odours – for example, cotton wool balls soaked in perfume, coffee beans, fresh lavender, cinnamon sticks, drinking chocolate and herbs

▶ a small funnel to help you to get the items into the bottles

▶ plastic glue such as UHU.

Reference to EYFS Development Statements

Knowledge and Understanding of the World: designing and making, page 81
0–11 months – Explore objects and materials with hands and mouth.

Creative Development: responding to experiences, page 108
8–20 months – Respond to what they see, hear, smell, touch and feel.

What and why

Babies are developing all their senses. This collection of bottles is linked to the important sense of smell.

Health warning: In very rare cases, some children may have an allergy to certain smells. Before starting this activity, check with parents and carers for any known instances and proceed with caution.

Before you start

Collect appropriate bottles for babies to use.

Gather all the smelly items that you intend to use and check that they are safe for the children to use. Ask parents and carers.

This is a 'dry' bottle collection – and therefore light for the baby to hold.

What to do:

1. Check that all labels have been removed from the bottles. Wash and clean them inside and out. Dry them thoroughly, especially inside.
2. From the collection of items, choose what to put in each bottle (coffee beans, lavender stems etc.). Stick to one smell per bottle – don't mix them.
3. Try each bottle by flipping up the drinking nozzle and squeezing the middle of the bottle. You should be able to smell what's inside.
4. Glue on the bottle cap with glue and wait until dry. Make sure you don't accidentally get glue on the nozzle!
5. Wipe each bottle thoroughly. Babies will put them in their mouths and some of the scents you have chosen may taste unpleasant.
6. Supervise this activity particularly carefully. Babies may need help squeezing the bottle to access the smell.
7. The life span of the contents will vary and some may need to be replenished or replaced at intervals. Check this collection yourself before each use and replace anything that smells unpleasant.
8. Ensure the bottles are cleaned with an antiseptic wipe after each use.

And another idea...

▶ Make a collection of soaps for babies to smell.
▶ Adapt to home cultures by using curry powder, coriander and other spices.
▶ Invite parents to bring a bottle to add to the collection.
▶ Put some natural perfumes in water play for babies to explore.
▶ Make or buy some small soft bags. Put smelly items in them and allow babies to hold the soft textured objects as well as exploring the smells.
▶ Use car fresheners – hang them as mobiles (out of reach) over the baby change area.
▶ Use scented stress balls in a small treasure basket.

Shake, Rattle and Roll

Make a bottle rattle for a baby toy

What you need:

▶ six or more clean bottles

▶ a collection of everyday items that make sounds when shaken – such as pasta, small keys, lentils, buttons, paper clips, rice, beads, small Lego bricks, little stones and glass beads

▶ a funnel – to help you to get the items in the bottles

▶ plastic glue such as UHU.

Reference to EYFS Development Statements

Knowledge and Understanding of the World: designing and making, page 81
0–11 months – Explore objects and materials with hands and mouth.

Creative Development: being creative: responding to experiences, page 108
0–11 months – Use movement and sensory exploration to connect with their immediate environment.

Creative Development: being creative: responding to experiences, page 108
8–20 months – Respond to what they see, hear, smell, touch and feel.

What and why

Babies are developing all their senses. This collection of bottles is linked to the important sense of hearing. Babies love shaking rattles and will enjoy the different sounds these bottles make.

Before you start

Try out all the objects and listen to the different sounds they make. Use metals as well as plastics and natural objects to get a good range of sounds. Aim for different pitches and tones. Some younger babies do not appreciate loud sounds, but usually, by the time they are 12 months old, they seek them!

What to do:

1. Check that all labels have been removed from the bottles. Wash and clean them inside and out. Dry them.

2. From your collection, choose items to put in each bottle. Fill them with varying quantities of the items you have chosen.

3. Test each bottle by shaking it and listening to the sound it makes. Does it make an interesting noise? Is it loud enough? Are the sounds clear? Are they varied?

4. When you are satisfied that there are enough items of the right kind in the bottles to stimulate the children, apply the glue to the necks of the bottles, screw on the lids, tighten and wait until dry.

5. Ensure the bottles are cleaned with an antiseptic wipe after each use.

And another idea...

▶ Fix a pine curtain pole or broom handle to the wall at baby height. Thread on bangles and rattles for the babies to play with.

▶ Make a sound treasure basket with everyday things that make a noise when moved, shaken or banged together.

▶ Hang items such as keys or small spoons on stretchy elastic above the nappy change area.

▶ Make 'pat mats' – small bags containing dried items that make different sounds and a different impact when patted and banged.

▶ Use the sound discovery bottles as an incentive to crawl. Ensure the bottles are the smooth round variety as they roll more easily. Have a shake, rattle and roll session with the babies!

Red for Go!

Primary colour bottles for babies

What you need:

I will need

▶ six or more clean bottles

▶ a collection of items all the same colour – for example, red items. You might collect red pompoms, red pegs, red pipe cleaners twisted in spirals, red artificial flowers and red buttons

▶ a funnel to help you to get items in the bottle

▶ plastic glue such as UHU.

Reference to EYFS Development Statements

Knowledge and Understanding of the World: designing and making, page 81
0–11 months – Explore objects and materials with hands and mouth.
Creative Development: responding to experiences, page 108
8–20 months – Respond to what they see, hear, smell, touch and feel.

What and why

Babies are often stimulated by colours. Offer items that are brightly coloured to excite and interest them. Start with red, blue and yellow. Add more colours as your collection grows.

Before you start

It is important to ensure that the bottles are clean and appropriate for the babies (not too heavy). Think about how the end products will be stored. Consider using a coloured trug or a container with a photograph of the bottles. Choose objects that will look good inside the bottles.

You might be able to find bottles with lids the right colours to match the contents.

What to do:

1. Wash the bottles inside and out. Ensure that labels and stickers are removed. Dry them.

2. Group items in their colours. Decide which colour to use for each bottle.

3. Fill the bottles with the items you have chosen – one colour per bottle. Fill one final bottle with a mixture of colours.

4. When you think that each bottle has enough items to stimulate the children, test them. Roll, twist and shake the bottles to see what happens. Try to make the collection varied so there are different effects.

5. Apply the glue to the necks of the bottles, screw on the lids, tighten and wait until dry.

6. Ensure the bottles are cleaned with an antiseptic wipe after each use.

And another idea...

▶ Spread a small parachute on the floor and put in each coloured segment the bottles that match that colour. Put the babies on the parachute so they can crawl and explore.

▶ See if you can get hold of some carpet or carpet tiles. Make, for example, a red carpet area by placing on it bottles that contain the red items. Do the same with blue, green and any other colours you've collected.

▶ Put some collage materials in a tough (builder's) tray for the babies to sit in and explore.

▶ Use drawstring bags containing collections of coloured items suitable for babies to play with.

▶ Give babies healthy snacks that are colour based, for example, oranges and carrots.

Moo Moo Meow Meow!

Animal bottles

What you need:

▶ six or more clean bottles, preferably with wide necks

▶ plastic models of animals – such as sheep, dogs, cats and ducks

▶ a small funnel to help you to get items in the bottles

▶ plastic glue such as UHU.

Reference to EYFS Development Statements

Knowledge and Understanding of the World: designing and making, page 81
0–11 months – Explore objects and materials with hands and mouth.

Creative Development: being creative and responding to experiences, page 108
8–20 months – Respond to what they see, hear, smell, touch and feel.

What and why

As babies begin to develop their language and their ability to distinguish and categorise items, they will start to recognise animals and to mimic the sounds that they make.

Before you start

Carry out some research on which animals appeal to the young babies in your care. For example, do they have contact with a domestic pet? How do they respond to the farmyard animals? Looking in baby books and showing them soft toys can be a starting point. Collecting animals of the right size to be squeezed into the bottles is a task in itself. It will help if you use bottles with the widest necks you can find.

What to do:

1. Wash the bottles inside and out. Ensure that labels and stickers are removed. Dry them.

2. Select the items to put in the bottles. For example, pocket money toys are cheap and these will be small enough to squeeze into the bottles. You may need to fold the legs to get them in, but it can be done if the plastic is soft enough.

3. Fill the bottles with varying quantities of the different animals. When you are satisfied that there are enough in each bottle to stimulate the children, try them out. Shake the bottles and observe the effect.

4. Apply the glue to the necks of the bottles, screw on the lids, tighten and wait until dry.

5. Ensure the bottles are cleaned with an antiseptic wipe after each use.

And another idea...

▶ Collect some soft toy animals that make the same sound (moo, growl, roar, bleat and bark). Keep them accessible to encourage follow-on play.

▶ Make collections of baby books that contain pictures of animals.

▶ Sing songs and rhymes about animals or featuring animal noises.

▶ Extend the range of the bottles. Start with domestic pets and farm animals, then move on to zoo animals and others.

▶ Fix some simple paper flaps on the wall. Beneath each, stick a picture of an animal so that the babies can lift and close the flaps to play peepkaboo with the animals!

Moving and shaking – toddlers and discovery bottles

Toddlers need to be stimulated as they explore their newly found mobility. All their senses are working intensely and they thrive on the new experiences offered to them. They enjoy playing with a variety of resources and these should be robust and safe.

Discovery bottles are an ideal resource for children at this stage. They can be developed to meet the needs of a toddler and they can be used inside and outside. It is important to think about the shape of the bottle for children in this age group. Smooth, cylindrical bottles move easily, rolling and spinning. The child will be stimulated to follow the bottle as it rolls away. Bottles with a square cross section are harder to move but may be easier to grab and hold. Both are useful, and thinking about the content of the bottle and how it will be used will help you to choose the right shape.

Make sure that the bottles are light enough for the children to pick up and play with easily. Larger bottles with heavier contents are suitable for use outside and sometimes offer a new challenge.

Toddlers are beginning to develop their observational skills and the contents of the discovery bottles will encourage language development. Remember when making and using your bottles that toddlers not only enjoy repetition but also need variety. Try to provide different opportunities to revisit, and practice skills and develop knowledge and understanding.

Make available some containers for bottles, such as milk bottle crates or bottle carriers (supermarkets usually have wine bottle carriers cheap or free and will often be pleased to give you some). The children will enjoy fitting the bottles into the slots, and it encourages one to one correspondence and early 'putting away' skills.

It will help you to organise your collections if you put some sticky labels on the bottle lids to identify them and to show which collection each bottle belongs to. These stickers are best avoided with bottles for babies because they may suck them, but they are usually fine with toddlers (use your discretion because even among these children, you may have some 'suckers' and 'chewers'!).

Some bottles have coloured lids and this offers a useful way of organising and identifying collections.

I Can See a Rainbow

Colour exploration for toddlers

What you need:

I will need

▶ at least seven (preferably more) plastic bottles, clean and dried

▶ collections of brightly coloured items – there are lots of possibilities. You might try:
yellow artificial flowers, red plastic cubes, blue pipe cleaners – twisted around a pencil to make spirals, orange buttons, green pompoms, purple plastic confetti (found in card shops – there are several different designs).

▶ a small jug

▶ a funnel or paper cone to help you to get the items into the bottles

▶ plastic glue such as UHU

▶ stickers – optional, but they will help you to organise your collections.

Reference to EYFS Development Statements

Creative Development: being creative, page 108
22–36 months – Seek to make sense of what they see, hear, smell, touch and feel.

Creative Development: being creative, page 110
30–50 months – Explore colour and begin to differentiate between colours.

What and why

Most children are fascinated by bright colours. The purpose of this activity is to make a set of bottles that relate to the different colours of the rainbow (red, orange, yellow, green, blue, indigo and violet). This will build on and extend the children's experience of colours.

Before you start

Collect a variety of items small enough to go in the bottles in as many colours of the rainbow as you can. Beads, buttons, coloured paper clips, coloured counters, small toys and wax crayons are all easy to obtain. Find or make some coloured stickers. Perhaps you can get hold of some rainbow stickers.

What to do:

1. Use bottles that are all the same size and shape, so that the colour is the focus. Wash the bottles inside and out. Ensure that labels and stickers are removed. Dry them.

2. Group the items you have collected in their different colours. Within each colour group, separate the items into 'wet' (i.e. those that are OK in water, for example, plastics) and 'dry' (i.e. those that are best kept dry, for example, paper).

3. Put the items in the bottles, one colour per bottle, keeping them in their separate wet and dry groups. Make sure you have enough in each bottle to make it interesting without overcrowding. Test the bottles by tipping and rolling them to see how the items move about inside.

4. When you're satisfied with the bottles, fill the 'wet' ones with water.

5. Stick the lids on the bottles using the glue. Tighten them up and leave them to dry.

6. Add coloured stickers.

And another idea...

▶ Label drawstring bags or boxes with the colours (use coloured stickers or the names of the colours written in the appropriate colour marker). Ask the children to put the bottles in the right bags/boxes.

▶ Add a few drops of food colouring to some of the bottles and observe what happens.

▶ Collect bottle tops of different colours and put them in a bag. Play a game by asking the children in turn to pick a top from the bag (without looking). If the colour they have chosen matches a bottle, they claim that bottle. The one who collects most bottles is the winner.

▶ Make a bottle shop in the imaginative play area.

Swirly Whirly

Bottles to move and shake

What you need:

I will need

▶ empty bottles (it will be more interesting if you can find a variety of shapes and sizes)

▶ a can of shaving foam

▶ food colouring (various colours)

▶ a small funnel

▶ patterned and coloured stickers (you can buy these or make your own on the computer)

▶ plastic glue such as UHU.

Reference to EYFS Development Statements

Creative Development: being creative, page 108
22–36 months – Seek to make sense of what they see, hear, smell, touch and feel.

Creative Development: being creative, page 110
30–50 months – Explore and experience using a range of senses and movements.

Creative Development: being creative, page 110
30–50 months – Explore colour and begin to differentiate between colours.

What and why

This activity uses shaving foam and food colouring to create stunning patterns and swirls of colour. These bottles should be made with the children (rather than prepared beforehand) so they can see the changes as the foam and various food colours are added. If tightly sealed, the bottles will be interesting for a few days, particularly if they're kept still, but don't expect them to last longer.

Before you start

Check the nozzle of the shaving foam is working. To avoid misuse and accidents, mark with a red pen where the foam comes out and explain this to the children.
Collect the bottles and make sure they are clean and absolutely dry (leave them on a warm radiator with their tops off for a few hours).

What to do:

1. Spray shaving foam into a bottle.

2. Add warm water to fill the bottle.

3. Put the lid on, shake the bottle and watch the foam dissolve.

4. When the foam has dissolved, take the top off and add some food colouring. You don't need much.

5. Apply glue, replace the lid and tighten it.

6. Watch the food colouring and the white foam swirl together. Move the bottle very gently, tilting and rolling to get the best effects.

And another idea...

▶ Experiment with different proportions of foam and food colouring. Talk about the differences using less water and more foam makes.

▶ Try adding a second colour. Then a third. What happens?

▶ Ask the children to make up some names for the bottles (for example, 'strawberries and cream', 'orange juice' and 'clouds and sky').

▶ Try some larger (2 litre) bottles. Does the foam/water/colour mixture behave differently?

▶ Use coloured foam for mark-making. Put the foam and food colouring in a washing-up bottle or sauce bottle and explore squirting the colour!

Pitter-Patter Raindrops

The sound of rain – in a bottle

What you need:

▶ an empty plastic bottle, clean and dry

▶ rice (uncooked)

▶ toothpicks or cocktail sticks (lollipop sticks are also suitable, and safer if you have any reservations about the children handling pointed sticks)

▶ a funnel or paper cone

▶ plastic glue such as UHU.

Reference to EYFS Development Statements

Communication, Language and Literacy: language for communication, page 44
22–36 months – Learn new words very rapidly and be able to use them in communicating about matters that interest them.

Knowledge and Understanding of the World: show curiosity and interest in the features of objects, page 79
22–36 months – Show an interest in why things happen.

Knowledge and Understanding of the World: show curiosity and interest in the features of objects, page 80
30–50 months – Show curiosity about why things happen and how things work.

Communication, Language and Literacy: linking sounds and letters, page 53
30–50 months – Enjoy rhyme and rhythmic activities.

What and why

Listening and responding to sounds gives toddlers the chance to do what they enjoy best – move and shake. This activity is designed to develop listening skills by encouraging listening and making sounds rhythmically. It also offers children opportunities to explore and carry objects around.

Before you start

Explore with the children the way the rice behaves and the sounds you can make with it. Tip it into a small plastic measuring jug. Let the children pour it from the jug over a plastic or metal tray (both if you can). Show the children the cocktail sticks and warn them about safety. If this is of concern, use lollipop sticks instead.

What to do:

1. Wash the bottles and leave the tops off to let them dry. Don't go on until you're sure they are thoroughly dry.

2. Take a clean, dry, empty bottle and pour in some of the rice. This is easier if you use a plastic jug and a funnel.

3. Add several toothpicks/cocktail sticks/lollipop sticks to the bottle.

4. Glue the lid onto the bottle. Leave it to dry.

5. Gently tilt and turn the bottle to get the sound of rain. Sing some songs about rain and use the bottle for the sound effects ('I Hear Thunder', 'Rain, Rain, Go Away', 'Raindrops Keep Falling on My Head' and 'Drip Drop Drip Little April Shower').

And another idea...

▶ Make some more rain bottles, using bottles of different sizes to get different sounds. Use them together in a 'rain band'.

▶ Make a thunder bottle by using marbles or glass stones, so that they swirl and make a louder sound.

▶ Make a tornado bottle, using screwed-up pieces of kitchen foil to create a different swirling effect.

▶ Make a snow bottle, which will have no sound, using small snowflake confetti.

A Story in a Bottle

A new look at traditional tales

What you need:

I will need

▶ three clean, dry, empty plastic bottles (the wider the tops, the better)

▶ three small plastic farmyard pigs (small enough to fit into the bottles)

▶ some twigs or very fine sticks

▶ straw, twigs or dried grass stalks (or strips of thin yellow card to represent straw)

▶ small bricks (for example, Lego)

▶ plastic glue such as UHU.

Reference to EYFS Development Statements

Communication, Language and Literacy: reading, page 55
22–36 months – Have some favourite rhymes, songs, poems or jingles.

Communication, Language and Literacy: reading, page 56
30–-50 months – Begin to be aware of the way stories are structured.

Problem Solving, Reasoning and Numeracy: numbers as labels and for counting, page 66
22–36 months – Have some understanding of one and two.

Problem Solving, Reasoning and Numeracy: numbers as labels and for counting, page 67
30–50 months – Use some number names accurately in play.

What and why

This activity combines storytelling with developing an understanding of number and exploring different materials. It will encourage children to join in the story and will help them with counting and number conservation.

Before you start

Read aloud or tell the story 'The Three Little Pigs'. If you're using an illustrated book, show the children the pictures so they can see the characters and scenery, and set the animals in context. If you're telling the story without a book, discuss with the children what each house might look like.

What to do:

1. Take the three bottles. Ensure they are thoroughly clean (no labels) and dry.

2. Put one plastic pig in each of the three bottles.

3. Tell the children that one bottle is for the straw house, one for the stick house and one for the house made of bricks. Let them help to choose what goes in each bottle – straw, sticks/twigs or bricks.

4. Glue the lids on the bottles.

5. Mark '1' on the lid of the straw bottle, '2' on the lid of the sticks bottle and '3' on the lid of the bricks bottle.

6. Read or tell the story again. Ask the children to indicate which bottle goes with each part of the story.

And another idea...

▶ If you can, get a plastic model of a wolf (an Alsatian dog will do) and let the children play out the story as you tell it.

▶ Try making bottles for some other stories featuring three characters – 'The Three Bears' and 'The Three Billy Goats Gruff'.

▶ Encourage the children to count for fun. Put some of their favourite objects in bottles, for example, dinosaurs, cars and small figures. Top up the bottle with sand or sawdust and ask them to find the figures and count how many.

▶ Help the children to make some bottles that represent the same number as their age. Stick a photograph of the child on the bottle. This makes a good birthday activity.

What's That Noise?

Being aware of, and recognising, sounds

What you need:

I will need

▶ empty plastic bottles – at least six. Clean and dry them thoroughly.

▶ a collection of small objects of different sizes, weights and densities, for example, lentils, beans, nuts and bolts, marbles, paper clips and uncooked rice. The aim is to find things small enough to fit into a plastic bottle that will make different sounds when shaken

▶ six socks

▶ a funnel

▶ plastic glue such as UHU.

Reference to EYFS Development Statements

Communication, Language and Literacy: linking sounds and letters, page 52
22–36 months – Distinguish one sound from another. Show interest in play with sounds, songs and rhymes.

Communication, Language and Literacy: linking sounds and letters, page 53
30–50 months – Show awareness of rhyme and alliteration

What and why

Listening to and distinguishing between sounds requires practice and experience. This activity will help children to develop the skills they will need later for distinguishing phonic sounds and general listening.

Before you start

Gather all the items you need to make the bottles.

Try out the items you have chosen to make sure there are noticeable differences in the sounds they make. Make sure that the socks cover the bottles and can be removed easily. Talk to the children about what you are going to do.

What to do:

1. Start with three plastic bottles. Check that each is clean, empty and dry.

2. Put in each bottle one of the sound items you have chosen (for example, lentils in one, marbles in another etc.).

3. Shake each bottle and listen to the sound it makes. Add or remove quantities until you're happy that the sound each bottle makes is clear and different from the others (put aside any that are too similar).

4. When you're satisfied, glue the lids onto the bottles.

5. Let the children see the bottles and try them, listening to the sounds they make and looking at the contents. Cover each bottle with a sock and mix them up. Shake them again and ask the children to say what's in each bottle.

And another idea...

▶ Make another set of bottles exactly the same as the first three, but this time add some water to each. Compare the sounds made by the wet set with those made by the dry set. Cover them all with socks and ask the children to say which is which.

▶ Think about songs that need sound effects (for example, 'I Hear Thunder'). Try to make some sound bottles that could be used to accompany these songs.

▶ Play some music and let the children accompany it with the sound bottles.

▶ March round and round to a rhyme, shaking the bottles as you go. This links physical movement to rhyme and rhythm, encouraging beat competence.

I Spy

Looking, wondering and talking

What you need:

▶ large, empty, clear plastic bottles. Be sure they are clean and dry

▶ salt, sand and uncooked rice – or you could use dried lentils or sago etc.

▶ a funnel

▶ a selection of five to ten small items, such as some small toys or crayons, cotton balls, five-pence pieces, counting bears, plastic animals, small dinosaurs, buttons, elastic bands etc. You need five to ten different things for each bottle

▶ plastic glue such as UHU

Reference to EYFS Development Statements

Knowledge and Understanding of the World: exploration and investigation, page 79
22–36 months – Show an interest in why things happen.

Knowledge and Understanding of the World: exploration and investigation, page 80
30–50 months – Describe and talk about what they see.

What and why

This activity encourages children to look carefully and find items. It helps to develop concentration, visual discrimination and extends language – all of which are important for toddlers as they begin to explore the world.

Before you start

Play the game 'I Spy' ('I spy with my little eye something that is round/blue/shiny etc.').
Talk about looking very carefully for things that are hidden.
Show the children the objects you are going to hide in the bottles. They need to see each one as a whole and uncovered in order to form pictures of them in their heads.

What to do:

1. Take the bottles and fill each with salt, rice or fine dry sand (there should be a variety of materials to look at – this encourages children to concentrate and discriminate).

2. Let the children watch and help you to insert the chosen objects into the bottles.

3. Seal the bottle lids with glue and allow to dry. Roll them around to bury the objects.

4. Get the children to tilt and shake the bottles to uncover the objects. Each time they find one they say, 'I spy a ...'. Let them see how many things they can spy, moving and shaking the bottles.

Tip: It's a good idea to note what was put in each bottle so you can support the toddler – they may insist there are only three items in the bottle when you know there are six!

And another idea...

▶ If you think your children need an easier start, begin with big bottles (for example, 1.5 or 2 litre drinks bottles) and larger objects.

▶ Hide the bottles outside and have a bottle hunt.

▶ Get hold of some coloured cellophane (for example, sweet wrappers) or lighting gels and look at the bottles through them, spying different colours.

▶ Try thickened liquids, such as flour and water paste, thick paint or even ready-made custard, to hide the objects.

Section Three

The latter stages of the Foundation Stage (3–5 year olds)

As children extend their knowledge and understanding of the world, their language develops. Their bodies grow and their hand/eye skills and their hand and finger grip improve. Children in this group will begin to be able to sequence simple events but may need lots of practical opportunities to reinforce this. Continuing practice with language and numbers is essential. Discovery bottles make excellent resources for the consolidation of counting and for activities based on saying and sounding letters.

As their independence in learning increases, children become capable of playing a greater part in designing and making their own discovery bottles. This gives plenty of opportunities for child-initiated learning. Please remember that even children in the later stages of the EYFS still need plenty of play-based experiences to promote and extend their learning, and it is important to give them the freedom and scope to construct bottles themselves and to use their imaginations in approaching the resources available and adapting them to their needs. Not only will constructing their own bottles support and extend their developing knowledge and experience, but it also offers opportunities for you to observe their degree of understanding. For example, investigating, experimenting with colours, mixtures and resources, and observing and making deductions are all examples of child-initiated activities, which can often be seen when children are working with discovery bottles. So throughout this section, make the bottles with the children, not for them, and allow them the space and freedom to take some control of the learning.

Discovery bottles offer a varied range of possibilities. They can be used to target specific knowledge and concepts; they can be employed out of doors to develop physical skills and an understanding of space and boundaries; they can be linked to stories, rhymes and artistic expression. Experimentation and construction using the materials suggested here contribute to the growth of scientific understanding and creative development. Activities with discovery bottles encourage children to be thinkers and inventors. This is the beauty of such a flexible resource, capable of being tailored to meet different needs and levels of learning.

An Alphabet Bottle

Using a bottle to help recognise letters

What you need:

> I will need

▶ empty, clear plastic bottles (rounded with no indents and preferably with wide necks). They should be clean and dry

▶ a range of objects each beginning with a specific sound. They should be small, easily recognisable and able to fit in a bottle. For example, for the 'b' sound, you could have a button, beads, a small bell, a plastic toy, a bear etc.

▶ coloured sand

▶ plastic glue such as UHU

▶ old or blank CDs (for presentation)

▶ a clipboard

▶ stickers

▶ pencils.

Reference to EYFS Development Statements

Communication, Language and Literacy: linking sounds and letters, page 52
22–36 months – Show interest in play with sounds, songs and rhymes.

Communication, Language and Literacy: linking sounds and letters, page 53
40–60+ months – Link sounds to letters, naming and sounding the letters of the alphabet.

What and why

Saying sounds and applying the knowledge of sounds through play makes learning words and letters fun. Some children are visual learners and need to see real objects. Some may wish to record items through drawing and writing.

Before you start

Decide which sound you are going to focus on. Gather some small objects which begin with that sound. Ensure the sound/object link is clear and will not confuse the children.

What to do:

1. Take a clear, empty plastic bottle. Make sure it is clean and thoroughly dry.

2. Part-fill the bottle with dry sand.

3. Insert the chosen items into the bottle. About six is enough to make the activity interesting without overwhelming the children.

4. Seal the bottle lid with glue. Let the glue dry, then roll the bottle to conceal the items.

5. To use the bottle, tilt it and shake it to uncover the items. As each object is found, ask the children to name it, emphasising the sound that starts it (for example, Bear).

6. Place a clipboard next to the bottle so that the children can record (draw) the items they find that begin with the chosen sound.

And another idea...

▶ Get children to make personal bottles by collecting objects that start with the same sound as their own name (for example, Carol – crisp, hair clip, model car, crayon; Patrick – pencil, paper, pin, paper clip, model pig etc.). N.B. Some children will need a lot of help with this. Finish off the bottle by sticking on it the child's name and a photograph.

▶ Try to make an alphabet of discovery bottles and line them up on a window sill or low shelf so they can be played with daily.

▶ Use the sand tray as a larger space and hide in it objects starting with the same letter – put another tray nearby with sand in for the children to practise the shape of the letter.

▶ Give more advanced children bottles containing objects representing two (or even more) sounds so that they have to sort and distinguish them – for example D and B.

Sizing Them Up

Practice in content and capacity

What you need:

I will need

▶ a collection of bottles of different shapes and sizes to use as a starting point and for children to use for free play and discussion

▶ empty plastic bottles – five or six of the same size and type for the task

▶ water and water play equipment (small measuring jugs, plastic tubing, funnels and pipettes)

▶ food colouring

▶ plastic glue such as UHU

▶ stickers.

Reference to EYFS Development Statements

Problem Solving, Reasoning and Numeracy: shape, space and measures, page 74
40–60+ months – Order two items by weight or capacity.

Problem Solving, Reasoning and Numeracy: shape, space and measures, page 75
40–60+ months – Sort familiar objects to identify their similarities and differences, making choices and justifying decisions.

What and why

Getting to grips with seriation (order) in mathematics and the language linked to capacity are important parts of mathematical development. It needs to be practical for young learners.

Before you start

For this activity, you need plenty of bottles of different shapes and sizes. Collecting them could include not only the children but also their families and other staff.
Waterproof aprons may be necessary and it's helpful to have towels at hand to dry children afterwards. Talk about the different sized bottles and how much they hold.

What to do:

1. Set up the plastic bottles, funnels, jugs and tubes in an area suitable for water play. This is an ideal activity for outside.

2. Ask the children to work carefully and to use the funnels and tubes to put water in their bottles (this will need to be a small group activity). Allow some free play before asking them to fill one bottle each. Let them choose how much water to put into their bottles.

3. Add a few drops of food colouring to each bottle.

4. Allow the children time to explore and experiment, to talk and to comment.

5. Seal the bottle lids with glue and leave them to dry.

6. When the glue is dry, put the bottles on a flat surface and mix them up.

7. Ask the children to put some of the bottles in order.

8. Photograph and record the process if appropriate.

And another idea...

▶ Focus on the colour green and find ten green plastic bottles. Ask for bottle number one to be full and bottle number ten to be empty. Can they make the quantity of water in the bottles in-between go down in small steps? When you have the set, sing the song 'Ten Green Bottles'.

▶ Use sand instead of water. Coloured sands behave very differently from water. The various colours could be layered.

▶ Provide large oven basters or plastic pipettes to use to transfer water into the bottles.

A Bottle Walk

Choosing and collecting

What you need:

I will need

▶ clear, wide-necked plastic bottles, clean and empty

▶ natural items found outside, in the grounds of the setting or in a park (leaves, conkers, berries, twigs, stones etc.)

▶ plastic glue such as UHU

▶ stickers

▶ pictures of natural items.

Reference to EYFS Development Statements

Knowledge and Understanding of the World: exploration and investigation, page 80
30–50 months – Show curiosity and interest in the features of objects and living things.

Knowledge and Understanding of the World: exploration and investigation, page 80
30–50 months – Describe and talk about what they see.

Knowledge and Understanding of the World: exploration and investigation, page 80
40–60+ months – Find out about, and identify, some features of living things, objects and events they observe.

What and why

Observing nature, talking about it and sharing observations is an important activity appropriate for many areas of the curriculum. It also presents good reasons for going out of doors. A bottle offers a convenient and safe way to study some natural objects. This activity is good for any time of the year, but it works particularly well in autumn.

Health and safety is particularly important in outdoor activities. Watch what children are picking up. Be aware of allergies. Warn children against putting things they find in their mouths and make sure they wash their hands as soon as they come inside.

Before you start

Going on a walk together is the ideal starter for this set of bottles. Plan the route beforehand and think about the things the children may find. It's a good idea to have books to hand for ideas and to help identify things.

What to do:

1. Ensure the plastic bottles are clean and dry.

2. Give each child or group an empty bottle to take on the walk. Explain that you are all going to collect some things to take back to remind them of the walk. The things they collect should be small enough to go into their bottle. Remind them to avoid collecting anything that moves.

3. Adults on the walk should help the children to choose what to collect and to drop their samples carefully into the bottles.

4. Make a display of the bottle collections. Ask the children to look at them and name the items that have been found.

5. The contents of the bottles won't keep indefinitely. Get the children to record their collections by drawing or photographing them.

Check to see whether there are any minibeasts in the bottles collected by accident (or even on purpose!). Let the children see any that are found but then release them and explain to the children why.

And another idea...

▶ Use empty CD cases instead of bottles. This introduces an additional selection criterion (the items collected must not only be very small but also flat).

▶ Encourage the children to make up some stories about the things they have collected.

▶ Make some bottle collections of flowers. Add a few drops of water and seal the bottles tight. Depending on the varieties, some of the flowers will last quite a long time (keep them cool and out of direct sunlight).

▶ In winter, fill the bottles with ice and frost, and watch the changes.

A Happy Bottle

Using bottles to start talking about feelings

What you need:

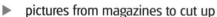

▶ plastic bottles – empty, clean and dry. Try to get those with brightly coloured tops

▶ the actual items needed for the bottles will depend on what the children suggest. You could offer buttons and confetti circles with smiles drawn on, bright feathers and a range of resources that you know the children like or enjoy using

▶ pictures from magazines to cut up

▶ plastic glue such as UHU

▶ smiley and sad face stickers.

Reference to EYFS Development Statements

Personal, Social and Emotional Development: dispositions and attitudes, page 27
30–50 months – Show increasing independence in selecting and carrying out activities.

Personal, Social and Emotional Development: dispositions and attitudes, page 27
30–50 months – Seek and delight in new experiences.

Personal, Social and Emotional Development: self-confidence and self-esteem, page 31
40–60+ months – Continue to be interested, excited and motivated to learn.

What and why

What makes you happy? The sunshine, a smiley face, a tickle with a feather?
The things we see have a strong impact on our feelings and emotions. This activity encourages children to be aware of feelings and to talk about them.

Before you start

Talk about what makes you happy and get the children to tell you things that make them happy. They might suggest listening to happy songs, being with their family or friends, going to a favourite place, having something new, their pets or things to eat.
This activity should engage children and there needs to be talking, laughing and sharing for it to succeed. Play music in the background to set a happy mood and to stimulate the children as they work.

What to do:

1. Gather enough bottles for each child or group to have one. They need to be clean and dry.

2. Tell the children you are going to make a 'happy bottle'. Ask them to suggest things to go in it.

3. Allow time for the children to choose and talk about the items they want in their happy bottle.

4. Collect the items to go into the bottles. This might take some time because it could involve bringing in things from home or outside the setting. Children can draw small pictures of things that are unsuitable for putting in the bottles, or cut pictures from the magazines.

5. When the collection is complete, seal the bottle lid. Add smiley stickers.

6. Sing 'If you're happy and you know it shake your bottle'!

And another idea...

▶ Try some other emotions, for example, a sad bottle or an angry bottle. What colours would they be?

▶ If you have a child presenting problem behaviour, use the bottle as a focus for their and your feelings and to give them a space to think about what they have done. Talk about how their behaviour makes others feel. Help them to make a calm bottle!

▶ Think of other songs that link to feelings and make bottles that reflect the moods of the songs.

Round and Round We Go!

Bottles for creative development

What you need:

- clear plastic bottles of various sizes, empty, clean and dry
- food colouring
- pieces of cloth or ribbons and fluffy pipe cleaners
- a collection of materials that move in interesting ways – small metallic balls, screwed-up foil, glitter (as many colours as you can find, but certainly gold and silver), polystyrene granules, confetti, beads, tinsel, ribbon etc.
- plastic glue such as UHU
- stickers and markers.

Reference to EYFS Development Statements

Creative Development: being creative, page 108
30–50 months – Capture experiences and respond to music, dance, paint and other materials or words.

Creative Development: exploring media and materials, page 112
40–60 months – Explore colour, texture, shape, form and space in two or three dimensions.

Creative Development: exploring media and materials, page 112
40–60 months – Explore what happens when they mix colours.

Creative Development: developing imagination and imaginative play, page 114
30–50 months – Enjoy joining in with dancing and ring games.

What and why

The aim here is to see what effects can be created by filling bottles with objects that move dramatically when spun. This gives opportunities both to explore the way materials behave and to respond to the effects created.

Before you start

Talk with the children about things that go round. Experiment with brightly coloured scarves swirled in the air, spinning tops and pipe cleaners wrapped round a pencil. Make a collection of brightly coloured objects so that there is a range of choices for children to explore and immerse themselves in. Items that are fluid and lend themselves to spinning, such as ribbons and strips of fabric, encourage children to twist and turn and explore the space around them.

What to do:

1. Take an empty plastic bottle and check that it is clean.
2. It's possible to make spinning bottles that contain dry objects or things floating in liquid. Start with a 'wet' bottle.
3. Explore and investigate the collection of materials available. Different coloured glitters in water make a good beginning. Fill the bottle with water and add a couple of teaspoons of glitter (maybe one spoonful of each colour).
4. Seal the bottle lid securely with glue.
5. Tilt and shake the bottle. Watch the glitter swirl. Now try spinning it.
6. Make up a swirly, spinning dance. See if you can find some swirly music to go with it (try 'Flight of the Bumble Bee', 'Tarantella', or make something up).

And another idea...

▶ Decorate the bottles using stickers and coloured markers.

▶ Try bottles of different sizes. Use large coke bottles and put pompoms inside them.

▶ Add food colouring to the water. Add baby oil. What difference does it make?

▶ Make some bottles with dry contents (coloured sand, confetti or polystyrene granules). Spin and roll the bottles to see what happens.

▶ Sit in a circle. Play a game: call out somebody's name and roll the bottle to them.

▶ Enhance the dance by tying ribbons onto wooden spoons and letting the children twist and turn with them in the air.

▶ Provide some bowls and get the children to explore round and round – use recipes that need stirring.

That Sinking Feeling

Exploring movement and space

What you need:

- a clean, empty plastic bottle. Use one with a wide neck
- a plastic tray
- a selection of small objects, some of which will float and some that will sink. Try to get plenty of each, including some that float just below the surface (to prompt discussion!)
- plastic glue such as UHU.

Reference to EYFS Development Statements

Knowledge and Understanding of the World: exploration and investigation, page 80
30–50 months – Show curiosity about why things happen and how things work.

Knowledge and Understanding of the World: exploration and investigation, page80
40–60+ months – Ask questions about why things happen and how things work.

What and why

Floating and sinking are concepts that fascinate children, as well as being important in understanding how objects behave. In this activity they experiment with what goes down in the bottle and sinks below the water level, and what stays above a water line. Up and down items can be very deceptive.

Before you start

Give plenty of free play experiences with water and a wide variety of natural and everyday objects, so children understand the differences between materials, and that something heavy doesn't necessarily sink. Spend time with the children exploring these objects and talking together about them.

What to do:

1. Fill a bottle with water until it's three quarters full (otherwise it will overflow when you put objects in the water).

2. Put a selection of the objects on a tray. Take one object at a time. Ask the children to hold it, feel it and weigh it in their hands. Ask them to guess whether it will float or sink.

3. Drop the chosen object carefully into the bottle and watch what happens. Was the prediction right?

4. Talk about what you've observed: what sinks, what floats and why?

5. Use more objects for thinking, estimating and testing in your 'float and sink' bottle.

And another idea...

▶ Add some baby oil to the water. Does it make any difference to what floats and what sinks?

▶ Find some things that sink slowly – talk about what is happening.

▶ Put some dolls in the water tray. Do they sink? How can you make them float?

▶ Experiment with things that float when you first put them in, then sink (try cotton wool, some fabrics or paper). Or offer things that dissolve, such as sugar.

▶ Pour dry materials (rice, lentils, ball bearings and sand) into the bottles and watch the effect. Use rollers and do large motor skills exercises up and down with paint.

Section Four

Song and rhyme bottles

Most children love songs and rhymes, and they play an important part in their development. Babies enjoy the repetition, which not only gives security but, as their understanding grows, encourages predicting and an appreciation of sounds. For older children, songs and rhymes play an important part in helping to prepare for reading. For all children, they support the development of beat competence, which we now know has a major correlation with all learning.

Each individual has a voice – not simply the sound made by their vocal chords, but the essence of their interaction with the world and a key component of personality. Starting to play with this voice is vital in developing both self-awareness and the skills of communication. Songs and rhymes are essential to this.

The bottles in this section are all connected with songs and rhymes. The bottle acts as a container for the props to illustrate or extend the song or rhyme. It also offers a way of getting children to focus on an activity either by looking at the bottle with them as you sing or say the rhyme, or by getting them to hold the bottle and use it as a prop. Older children will have built up their own repertoire of songs and rhymes that they love, so for them there is the challenge of finding items for their own bottles and linking them to a favourite song or rhyme.

Song and rhyme bottles can provide spontaneous opportunities for children to sing and say rhymes on their own or can be used in group times. The idea is that the bottle encourages singing or saying the rhyme and that the props help to remind children of the ideas, rhymes and characters.

There is space here to cover only a limited amount of material. There are many suitable songs and rhymes, and using appropriate cultural rhymes may stimulate further ideas. This section is designed to get you started and encourage you to begin thinking about songs that children sing, or songs you know yourself that you want to share with the children in your setting. Creating new rhymes too is important, as this encourages children to experiment and play with words.

Songs and rhymes can be used by anyone. Do not feel you have to possess particular skills. You do not need to be an accomplished singer, speaker or musician – just have a go. Enjoy singing and let the children see you as a role model so that they will join in and enjoy it too.

Incy Wincey Spider

At home with the creepy crawlies

What you need:

▶ clear plastic bottles, empty and clean

▶ a collection of small pebbles or gravel that has been washed in a colander

▶ fine garden netting (for example, raspberry netting, or you could collect the netting used to contain oranges or other fruit when sold in a supermarket)

▶ a small funnel (may help you to get items into the bottle)

▶ small plastic spiders from a toy, joke or craft shop

▶ plastic glue such as UHU

▶ stickers.

Reference to EYFS Development Statements

Knowledge and Understanding of the World: exploring and investigation, page 79
0–11 months – Use movement and senses to focus on, reach for and handle objects.

Physical Development: using equipment and materials, page 103
16–26 months – Begin to make and manipulate objects and tools.

Knowledge and Understanding of the World: exploring and investigation, page 80
30–50 months – Show curiosity and interest in the features of objects and living things.

Communication, Language and Literacy: language for communication, page 48
40–60+ months – Listen with enjoyment, and respond to stories, songs and other music, rhymes and poems.

What and why

This is a well-known rhyme and children will be fascinated watching the spiders descend through the netting. Some of them will grip and cling to the netting, and the gravel creates a sound too. This bottle is a mini-environment and children will love to have time to look and talk about it as well as sing the song.

Before you start

Make sure that the children are familiar with the song 'Incy Wincey Spider' and the actions that go with it. Sing it together a few times, using hands and fingers. Gather the resources and ensure all the items are available.

What to do:

1. It's best to use a larger (1.5 or 2 litre) bottle for this activity. Start by putting a layer of the clean gravel at the bottom of the bottle.

2. Cut a piece of the netting to the size of a small handkerchief and push it into the bottle so that it sits just above the gravel.

3. Carefully pour water into the bottle until it covers the gravel by 5–6 cm.

4. Gently tip the spiders into the bottle. They will cascade down the inside.

5. Seal the lid on the bottle with the glue, tighten and wait until dry.

6. Shake the bottle to make the spiders move around in the netting. Sing 'Incy Wincey Spider' while you do.

Remember that not everyone likes spiders – so be sensitive to the feelings of children and other adults.

And another idea...

▶ Using one of the spiders, can you make a bottle for 'Little Miss Muffet'?

▶ Talk about spiders and their value in trapping flies, wasps and mosquitoes. Look for spiders' webs and nests in the garden and around the setting.

▶ Make a spider's home in a bottle. What are you going to put in it? (N.B. Use a plastic spider, not a real one!)

▶ Sing 'Incy Wincey Spider' again and make up a spidery dance.

Five Little Ducks went Swimming One Day

Counting and singing as the ducks go swimming

What you need:

I will need

▶ a clean, empty bottle with no labels. Try to get one with a wide neck and without ribs so that the things you put into the bottle can move around

▶ five small plastic ducks. If you can't get farmyard models, draw duck shapes on buttons in indelible marker

▶ water and blue food colouring (or dip blue crêpe paper in the water to colour it)

▶ some plastic greenery from an aquarium shop or craft shop

▶ plastic glue such as UHU.

Reference to EYFS Development Statements

Communication, Language and Literacy: linking sounds and letters, page 52
16–26 months – Listen to and enjoy rhythmic patterns in rhymes and stories.

Communication, Language and Literacy: reading, page 55
16–26 months – Show an interest in stories, songs and rhymes.

Problem Solving, Reasoning and Numeracy: calculating, page 69
22–36 months – Know that a group of things changes in quantity when something is added or taken away.

Communication, Language and Literacy: language for communication, page 48
40–60+ months – Listen with enjoyment, and respond to stories, songs and other music, rhymes and poems.

56

What and why

All children will enjoy this well-known rhyme, and younger ones will particularly like the sound when mother ducks says 'quack, quack'. For older children, it provides a good opportunity for simple subtraction.

Before you start

Make some bigger ducks available for play.
Use a water tray so that the idea of the ducks floating along becomes established and is experienced first hand. Use some blue cloth and the greenery to represent the water and artificial grass. Younger children will have a lot of fun with this.

What to do:

1. Check the bottle is clean, is free from labels and that the lid seals well (it's going to have to hold water).

2. Place the bottle on its side. Put a thin layer of clean gravel (4–5 cm) in the bottom of the bottle.

3. Tilt the bottle onto its side. Take small amounts of the greenery and push them into the bottle so they sit on top of the gravel.

4. Tilt the bottle and pour the coloured water in gently, through the greenery and onto the gravel.

5. Place the ducks in the bottle.

6. Glue the lid firmly onto the bottle and wait until dry.

7. The bottle can be shaken or rolled, but when you put it down on its side again, the gravel will return to the bottom of the bottle, and the ducks will float on the top of the water.

8. Sing the song together.

And another idea...

▶ Put three pretend mice (found in pet shops in the cat toy section) into a large bottle with some props. Sing 'Three Blind Mice'.

▶ Put some cotton wool or wadding into a large bottle with five small plastic monkeys. Shake the bottle and sing together 'Five Little Monkeys Jumping on the Bed'.

▶ Think about other environments that could be used for small plastic animals, for example, try using small stones and some dinosaurs, or a different sort of greenery with twigs and monkeys. Try to make up a song to fit.

Here We Go Round the Christmas Tree

Bottles for festivals and events

What you need:

▶ a large, clean bottle with the labels removed. Try to get one without ribs or other indentations so that the items inside can move around freely

▶ quick-drying, waterproof glue

▶ a stick or piece of dowel about 10 cm longer than the bottle.

▶ Blu-tac and glitter

▶ a small model Christmas tree that can be fitted through the neck of the bottle. The sort used for cake decorations is ideal, or use a small plastic fir tree from a model shop

▶ Christmas stickers

▶ water and plastic glue such as UHU.

Reference to EYFS Development Statements ———————

Communication, Language and Literacy: linking sounds and letters, page 52
16–26 months – Listen to and enjoy rhythmic patterns in rhymes.

Communication, Language and Literacy: reading, page 55
16–26 months – Show an interest in stories, songs and rhymes.

Communication, Language and Literacy: language for thinking, page 50
30–50 months – Talk activities through, reflecting on and modifying what they are doing.

Knowledge and Understanding of the World: communities, page 90.
40–60+ months – Begin to know about their own cultures and beliefs, and those of others.

What and why

This activity focuses on the Christmas tree and singing a nursery rhyme. The idea can be adapted for other festivals and events.

Before you start

To allow children to have a first-hand experience, get them to hold hands and dance around a tree. It can be a tree in the outdoor area (and you can sing 'Here we go round the ... tree', or if you have a Christmas tree indoors, you could use that.

What to do:

(N.B. Stage 3 is for adults only – keep the children away from the glue.)

1. Leave the bottle on a radiator or beside a heater to ensure that it's completely dry (not too hot or it will melt and go out of shape!).

2. Place the bottle upright.

3. Use a large piece of Blu-tac to fix the top of the model tree on the end of the stick or dowel. Put a dab of the quick-drying glue on the base of the tree and use the stick to position it on the bottom of the bottle. Allow to dry. (You might want to practise doing this without the glue first, just so you get the hang of it.)

4. Fill the bottle with water. Add some glitter to the bottle – not too much, about a teaspoonful will do.

5. Add some small stars and/or Christmas confetti if you wish. Add a little at a time and look at the effect.

6. Screw on the lid and tighten. You may want to glue it to make it waterproof.

7. The bottle can be shaken and rolled – the idea is to create the magic feel of Christmas as the glitter swirls round the tree. Try singing:

> Here we go round the Christmas tree
> The Christmas tree, the Christmas tree.
> Here we go round the Christmas tree,
> On a cold and frosty morning.

And another idea...

▶ You can make an Easter bottle (using small fluffy chickens), a 5 November one (how could you do the fireworks?) or a Halloween one (but be aware of religious and cultural sensibilities).

▶ Make a Diwali bottle – using bindis (Indian decorations for the forehead) and coloured water – to celebrate the Hindu festival.

▶ Celebrate the Chinese New Year. Make a bottle using dragons and streamers cut from coloured plastic bags. Play some Chinese music and dance with your bottle.

▶ These bottles make great festival items for children to take home. They can choose the contents and add water and glitter.

Party time

A bottle to celebrate a birthday

What you need:

I will need

▶ a large, clean bottle with the labels removed. Try to get one without ribs or other indentations – so that the items inside can move around freely

▶ glitter

▶ water

▶ birthday cake decorations (candles, plastic numbers, stars etc.)

▶ party stickers

▶ plastic glue such as UHU.

Reference to EYFS Development Statements

Knowledge and Understanding of the World: communities, page 89
22–36 months – Have a sense of their own immediate family and relations.

Personal, Social and Emotional Development: dispositions and attitudes, page 26
30–50 months – Have a positive approach to activities and events.

Knowledge and Understanding of the World: communities, page 90
30–50 months – Express feelings about a significant personal event.

Knowledge and Understanding of the World: page 90
40–60+ months – Feel a sense of belonging to their own community and place.

What and why

Most months, there'll be a child in your setting or group who is having a birthday. A birthday bottle is a great way to celebrate and provides opportunities for individual and group work, and for language development.

Before you start

Keep an up-to-date calendar or display which will remind you of the birthdays and, if necessary, ages or dates of birth. Make it a feature and look at it with the children. Assuming they have been involved in making and/or playing with some discovery bottles before, ask them to suggest what you could put into a birthday bottle.

What to do:

1. Decide whose birthday you are going to celebrate and establish how old they are.

2. Make sure that the bottle is clean and dry. Assemble all the items you are going to use.

3. Place the bottle upright. Start by putting in the larger items, such as a birthday candle and the birthday number (let the children pick it out from a selection). Tell them, 'This is Nathan's (or Julie's or whoever's) birthday bottle. We've put in a candle and their birthday number. Now we need to add some of their favourite things.' Ask the children to suggest items to add (for example, plastic model animals, small toys etc.).

4. Fill the bottle with water.

5. Gently tip the glitter into the bottle. Add some birthday confetti (sold in card shops). Glue the lid onto the bottle, tighten it and wait until dry.

6. If you can, complete the bottle by sticking a photograph of the birthday boy or girl on the bottle. If you have a digital camera, perhaps the children can take one specially.

Over several months, you should be able to make a birthday bottle for everyone. Make a display of them. Be sure that children who have birthdays at weekends or when the setting is closed don't miss out!

And another idea...

▶ Get the children to make birthday bottles for parents, grandparents (the numbers might be a challenge!), brothers or sisters.

▶ If someone in the group has a newborn brother or sister, you could make a baby birthday bottle.

▶ Instead of 'Pass the Parcel', play 'Pass the Bottle', using a lucky dip as a prize.

▶ Make bottles for other significant events, such as marriages or christenings.

Row, Row, Your Boat

A whole bottle workout

What you need:

I will need

▶ large, clean bottles with the labels removed. Try to get them without ribs or other indentations, so that the items inside can move around freely. Ideally you need one bottle for each child

▶ fine aquarium gravel

▶ small shells and plastic greenery

▶ a small plastic boat (small enough to go into the bottle)

▶ water and some blue food colouring (or dip blue crêpe paper in the water to colour it)

▶ plastic glue such as UHU.

Boats

Reference to EYFS Development Statements

Communication, Language and Literacy: linking sounds and letters, page 52
16–26 months – Listen to and enjoy rhythmic patterns in rhymes.

Physical Development: movement and space, page 95
22–36 months – Respond to rhyme, music and story by means of gesture and movement.

Communication, Language and Literacy: linking sounds and letters, page 53
30–50 months – Enjoy rhyming and rhythmic activities.

What and why

This is a whole-body action song, linked with the traditional idea of a boat in a bottle. It's best if the children have a bottle each. They can then 'row' with them, singing as they go.

Before you start

Children need a warm-up before embarking on large motor skills and a cool down afterwards. Warm the children up by getting them to sit down and do some stretches. Follow this by encouraging them to touch their toes and put their arms by their sides, waving them up and down.

What to do:

1. Check that the bottles are clean and that the lids seal well (the bottles will be holding water).
2. Tip the bottle on its side and squirt some glue on the inside (for the bottom of the sea).
3. Tip gravel into the bottle and swirl it so that it sticks to the glue. Add the gravel a little at a time and don't use too much. The idea is to have just enough gravel to mix with the glue so that it will stick on the side of the bottle (see illustration). Put the bottle aside until the glue is thoroughly dry (at least overnight).
4. Put the boat into the bottle. If there is a mast or sails, you may have to squeeze them down.
5. Add the shells and greenery.
6. Fill the bottle about half full with the coloured water.
7. Seal the lid with glue.
8. Tip the bottle on its side to make the boat float.

And another idea...

▶ Use the bottles as skittles and see how many you can knock down.
▶ Make a line of five bottles (ten with older children). Sing 'Five Green Bottles', removing a bottle each time.
▶ Make some different water scenes. You can use plastic fish, shipwrecks and divers. Tropical fish sections of garden centres are a good source.

Ring a Ring o' Roses

A song and rhyme bottle

What you need:

I will need

▶ large, clean bottles with the labels removed. Try to get them without ribs or other indentations, so that the items inside can move around freely. Ideally you need one bottle for each child

▶ some small plastic roses (or other flowers – any will do)

▶ glue, wire or string to fix the flowers together

▶ water.

Reference to EYFS Development Statements

Communication, Language and Literacy: linking sounds and letters, page 52
16–26 months – Listen to and enjoy rhythmic patterns in rhymes and stories.

Physical Development: movement and space, page 95
22–36 months – Respond to rhyme, music and story by means of gesture and movement.

Creative Development: creating music and dance, page 114
30–50 months – Enjoy joining in with dancing and ring games.

What and why

This is a traditional rhyme, which many of the children will know. They will love to join in, holding hands and falling down as they sing the song. This will develop listening and a sense of rhythm. The need to avoid others when falling will develop spatial awareness and help with control of movement.

Warning: this game can become quite wild!

Before you start

Play some circle games. Practice moving and singing the songs at the same time. Develop a repertoire of circle rhymes and games for outside.

What to do:

1. Check that the bottle is clean and that the lid seals well (this bottle will be holding water).

2. Fix the roses together in a 'daisy chain', using glue, fine wire or string. Keep quick-setting glue (for example, 'Superglue') away from children.

3. Carefully push the chain of roses through the top of the bottle.

4. Fill the bottle with water and seal the top on with glue.

5. Decorate the bottles with stickers if you wish.

6. Place the bottles in a circle on the floor. You could display them on silver CDs or coasters to enhance the presentation.

7. The children can move round the bottles, alone or with help (according to their ages and stages, and what they can do), singing 'Ring a Ring o' Roses'. When you get to 'we all fall down' the children collapse, knocking the bottles over as they do so!

Remember, songs, rhymes and movement go together for the active learner!

And another idea...

▶ Put the bottles in a random pattern around the room and weave in and out of them as you sing.

▶ Play the game again, but this time the object is to avoid knocking the bottles over. (You might like to start with this!)

▶ Make some other bottles based on rhymes and movement games (for example, 'Oranges and Lemons', 'What Time is it Mr Wolf?', 'The Big Ship Sails' and 'Here We Go Round the Mulberry Bush').

Smelly Bottles

This section concentrates on smells. Children need to experience a range of smells and using discovery bottles is one way this can be done in a hygienic and safe way. Herbs, perfumes and foods inside the bottles will provide a range of odours for children to explore and talk about.

For these activities, you need to collect some sports 'shooter' drinking bottles with nozzles in the lids. If you squeeze the bottle sharply, the air forced out of it will carry the smell of whatever is in the bottle. This property can be used to develop and focus the sense of smell, to challenge the imagination and to link the sense of smell with language.

Some sports bottles are clear and you can see the contents. Others are made of coloured plastic and the contents cannot be seen. Collect both sorts and, after they've had some experience, use non see-through bottles and get the children to guess what's inside them. Using smaller bottles will control the amount of air passed through the nozzle.

'Scratch and Sniff' features have been incorporated into books for young children and this idea can be built on to provide a wider range of sensory experiences.

The different ranges of smells may trigger memories and connect events or people in your brain, even as an adult.

Health and safety warning

Babies can experience 'smelly' bottles safely. However, it is important for practitioners to be aware of the dangers of allergies and to know the details of any children in their care who are allergic. Even minor exposure can trigger an allergic reaction, and a very small number of children have such sensitive health problems that these activities would be inappropriate and possibly dangerous for them. Always check before embarking on the activity.

Chill Out

Using smells to feel calm

What you need:

▶ a clean, dry bottle. This must be a sports or shooter bottle so that air can be squeezed out to carry the smell of the contents

▶ fresh or dry lavender

▶ plastic glue such as UHU

▶ purple stickers.

Reference to EYFS Development Statements

Creative Development: being creative, page 108
8–20 months – Respond to what they see, hear, smell, touch and feel.

Creative Development: being creative, page 108
22–36 months – Seek to make sense of what they see, hear, smell, touch and feel.

Personal, Social and Emotional Development: disposition and attitudes, page 27
30–50 months – Seek and delight in new experiences.

Creative Development: being creative, page 108
40–60+ months – Respond in a variety of ways to what they see, hear, smell, touch and feel.

What and why

This is a smell that many people find soothing. Fresh lavender can be picked from the garden or bought at markets and various shops. The song 'Lavender's Blue' makes a good accompaniment. This calming bottle can be used when the children (and you!) will benefit from some peace and quiet.

Before you start

Harvest or source the lavender. Try to involve the children in this – not all children will connect this smell to a plant, so touching and exploring the lavender is an essential part of the learning before it is placed in the bottle.

What to do:

1. Place the bottle upright.
2. Put some lavender in the bottle. You'll need to experiment to get the right amount – enough to produce a reasonably strong smell when the bottle is squeezed.
3. Seal the lid with glue.
4. Add stickers and a picture of lavender if you can get one.
5. Squeeze the centre of the bottle gently and test the aroma! Sing the song 'Lavender's Blue', calm the children down and r-e-l-a-x.

   Lavender's blue, dilly, dilly, lavender's green,

   When I am king, dilly, dilly, you shall be queen.

   Who told you so, dilly, dilly, who told you so?

   'Twas my own heart, dilly, dilly, that told me so.

And another idea...

▶ Harvest some other traditional plants. Most herbs will be suitable (try sage, rosemary or thyme). Note the different textures and smells.

▶ Use some dried spices. Chinese and Indian shops have a wide range of these.

▶ Buy some fresh herbs at the supermarket. Cutting releases the scents, so use scissors to cut them before placing them in the bottles.

Soap Scents

Super clean smells in a bottle

What you need:

I will need

▶ a clean, dry bottle. This must be a sports or shooter bottle so that air can be squeezed out to carry the smell of the contents

▶ several bars of different smelling soaps. Choose strong smelling or fruity soaps. Cheap soap usually smells strongest!

▶ a kitchen grater (plastic, not metal)

▶ plastic glue such as UHU

▶ stickers

▶ a funnel may be helpful for putting the flakes into the bottle.

Reference to EYFS Development Statements

Creative Development: being creative, page 108
8–20 months – Respond to what they see, hear, smell, touch and feel.

Creative Development: being creative, page 108
22–36 months – Seek to make sense of what they see, hear, smell, touch and feel.

Creative Development: being creative, page 108
40–60+ months – Respond in a variety of ways to what they see, hear, smell, touch and feel.

What and why

Soap offers a simple and easy source of strong and pleasant smells. Washing is an everyday routine that ensures we keep our bodies clean. Using a grater may be new to some children.

Before you start

Spend some time smelling and talking about the soaps. Ask which they like. If appropriate, use this as an opportunity to talk to the children about the importance of cleanliness. Older children may be interested in how soap is made.

What to do:

1. Decide how many bottles you are going to make and choose enough soaps. Three is a good start and it's best if you can find soaps with very different smells.

2. Use the grater to make a small pile of soap shavings from each of the three bars. Keep the piles of shavings separate from each other.

3. Fill each bottle with one of the piles of shavings.

4. Seal the lid of each bottle securely with glue.

5. Test the bottle by giving the middle a squeeze. The idea is to make a sudden short puff of air.

6. Let the children experiment with the bottles. Ask them to close their eyes to see if they can tell the difference between the soap scents.

And another idea...

▶ See how many different soapy smells you can collect.

▶ Give each bottle a number. Allow the children time to play with the bottles and learn which smell goes with which number. Play a game. Conceal the numbers and ask the children to smell the bottles and say which is which.

N.B. All soaps sold for domestic use are safe. However, they taste nasty and sting if you get them in your eyes. Warn the children not to rub their eyes or lick their fingers if they've been helping by handling the soap bars or shavings.

Spicy Scents

Teatime smells from a simple spice

What you need:

I will need

▶ a clean, dry bottle. This must be a sports or shooter bottle so that air can be squeezed out to carry the smell of the contents

▶ cinnamon sticks and very small amounts of cinnamon powder

▶ a funnel to help fill the jar

▶ plastic glue such as UHU

▶ stickers and coloured markers.

Reference to EYFS Development Statements

Creative Development: being creative, page 108
8–20 months – Respond to what they see, hear, smell, touch and feel.

Creative Development: being creative, page 108
22–36 months – Seek to make sense of what they see, hear, smell, touch and feel.

Creative Development: being creative, page 108
40–60+ months – Respond in a variety of ways to what they see, hear, smell, touch and feel.

What and why

The pungent fragrance of cinnamon* is unmistakable, usually evoking dreams of hot cinnamon rolls from the oven. This spicy smell is very different from the aromas of the herbs used in the first activity in this section. Helping children to become aware of the difference will develop their sense of smell and their recognition of smells. Get them to respond by using language to describe the smells.

*One study found that smelling cinnamon boosts cognitive function and memory.

Before you start

Getting hold of the cinnamon may require a trip to the supermarket, market or local shops. Make this a part of the activity. The smells of many small multi-cultural shops (Asian, Chinese and West Indian) are an experience in themselves. If you are using powdered cinnamon, a funnel may help when transferring it to the bottle.

What to do:

1. Make sure the bottle is clean and dry.
2. Put a few cinnamon sticks and/or a small amount of powdered cinnamon into the bottle, using the funnel.
3. Seal the lid but don't glue it yet. Test the strength of the aroma and add more sticks or powder if necessary (the powder smells more strongly than the sticks).
4. When you're satisfied, glue the lid in place.
5. Decorate the bottle if you wish – use stickers and pictures or draw directly onto the bottle with coloured markers.
6. Let the children play and experiment with the scent of cinnamon. Ask them to talk about the smell and what it makes them think of.

And another idea...

▶ Make another bottle using ginger (grate raw ginger into the bottle or use powdered ginger). Get some ginger biscuits and let the children taste them. Let them experience the difference between the smell and the taste of ginger.

▶ Use cloves – these are often used to ease colds and so have a strong aroma too.

▶ Try some recipes using cinnamon, ginger or cloves.

Health and safety

If you're using powdered cinnamon, it's important to squeeze the bottle gently and not directly into faces. If the bottle is squeezed too hard, the powder may puff out, making people sneeze and stinging their eyes. Warn the children about this.

DO NOT use chilli powder or peppers of any sort.

Putting spices into the bottles is an adult activity; children may rub their eyes after using the powder and this will sting!

If you are unsure about this activity, use whole spices, lightly crushed, instead of powdered or ground spices.

Wake Up and Smell the Coffee

An everyday smell with widespread appeal

What you need:

▶ a clean, dry bottle. This must be a sports or shooter bottle so that air can be squeezed out to carry the smell of the contents

▶ coffee beans and freshly ground coffee – get this in a vacuum pack, so you can replace it when the smell wears off

▶ a funnel

▶ plastic glue such as UHU

▶ stickers and coloured markers.

Reference to EYFS Development Statements

Creative Development: being creative, page 108
8–20 months – Respond to what they see, hear, smell, touch and feel.

Creative Development: being creative, page 108
22–36 months – Seek to make sense of what they see, hear, smell, touch and feel.

Creative Development: being creative, page 108
40–60+ months – Respond in a variety of ways to what they see, hear, smell, touch and feel.

What and why

Coffee has a very particular smell and most children will know it. For younger children, recognising and responding to the smell will be enough, while for older ones, it will provide an opportunity to learn about where coffee comes from.

Before you start

Talk about coffee. Who drinks coffee in their homes?
Go shopping for the coffee. Let children feel the beans and the powder. Talk about how the beans become powder. You might be able to grind some coffee while the children watch (this makes a special aroma too). If you have a local delicatessen that roasts coffee on the premises, you may be able to visit. With older children, show some pictures to illustrate how and where coffee is grown.

What to do:

1. Take two bottles. Make sure both are clean and dry.
2. Put the coffee beans in one bottle and the ground coffee in the other (instant coffee will do instead of ground coffee).
3. Screw on the lids but don't glue them yet. Test the strength of the aroma and add more coffee if necessary.
4. When you're satisfied, glue the lids in place.
5. Decorate the bottles if you wish – use stickers and pictures or draw directly onto the bottle with coloured markers.
6. Let the children play and experiment with the smell of coffee. Ask them to talk about the smell and what it makes them think of.

And another idea...

▶ Make coffee play dough using granules of coffee in the mixture. This will allow the colour and smell of the coffee to be experienced in another way.

▶ Make a cup of coffee and let the children taste a small amount. They probably won't like it – particularly without milk and sugar.

N.B. Coffee is a stimulant, so only let them taste a little. Some parents may have strong views about children tasting any stimulant, even in very small quantities. Tell parents what you want to do and check it with them first.

Chocolate Heaven!

A chance to experiment with everybody's favourite food

What you need:

▶ a clean, dry bottle. This must be a sports or shooter bottle so that air can be squeezed out to carry the smell of the contents.

▶ cocoa powder

▶ a funnel

▶ plastic glue such as UHU.

Reference to EYFS Development Statements

Creative Development: being creative, page 108
8–20 months – Respond to what they see, hear, smell, touch and feel.

Creative Development: being creative, page 108
22–36 months – Seek to make sense of what they see, hear, smell, touch and feel.

Creative Development: being creative, page 108
40–60+ months – Respond in a variety of ways to what they see, hear, smell, touch and feel.

What and why

The aroma of chocolate is unmistakable. The botanical name for cocoa is 'Theobroma Cacao'; Theobroma means 'God food'!

Before you start

A very small number of children are allergic to chocolate. It is also bad for some medical conditions. Check this with parents before you start.

Talk about favourite tastes and smells. Get some examples of the many different forms chocolate takes. Talk about these and maybe taste some of them.

With older children, talk about where cocoa comes from and how chocolate is made.

What to do:

1. Make sure the bottle is clean and dry.
2. Pour some cocoa powder into the bottle using the funnel.
3. Seal the lid but don't glue it yet. Test the strength of the aroma and add more cocoa powder if necessary.
4. When you're satisfied, glue the lid in place.
5. Decorate the bottle if you wish – use stickers and pictures or draw directly onto the bottle with coloured markers.
6. Let the children play and experiment with the smell. Ask them to talk about the smell and what it makes them think of.

And another idea...

▶ Make a tea bottle, using powdered lemon tea for a citrus smell.

The Scent of Flowers

The many different aromas of pot-pourri

What you need:

▶ some clean, dry bottles. They must be sports or shooter bottles so that air can be squeezed out to carry the smell of the contents

▶ some samples of pot-pourri. There are many sorts, so try to get four very different ones

▶ it may be helpful to have some pot-pourri oils too, to refresh the bottles when the scents begin to fade

▶ a funnel.

Reference to EYFS Development Statements

Creative Development: being creative, page 108
8–20 months – Respond to what they see, hear, smell, touch and feel.

Creative Development: being creative, page 108
22–36 months – Seek to make sense of what they see, hear, smell, touch and feel.

Creative Development: being creative, page 108
40–60+ months – Respond in a variety of ways to what they see, hear, smell, touch and feel.

What and why

The practice of bringing plant petals, seeds and roots indoors to perfume a room is ancient. Using pot-pourris gives children the chance to experience and respond to a range of scents.

Before you start

If you can, take the children with you to choose the pot-pourri.

Tip out some of the pot-pourri samples onto small trays or saucers. Let the children smell them. Let them examine and feel the different textures. Be careful not to mix the samples up.

What to do:

1. Make sure all the bottles are clean and dry.

2. Put a sample of pot-pourri in each bottle, one per bottle.

3. Screw the bottle lids on tightly but don't glue them (you may want to add pot-pourri oils to refresh the samples later).

4. Decorate the bottles if you wish – use stickers and plant pictures or draw directly onto the bottle with coloured markers.

5. Let the children play and experiment with the smells. Get them to talk about the smells and what they make them think of. Ask them to choose their favourite.

And another idea...

▶ There are a lot of pot-pourri mixes available. They often have mood names, or are called after the seasons. Ask the children to make up their own names for some of them.

▶ Use an appropriate pot-pourri as part of a seasonal celebration – spring, Christmas and so on.

▶ Use clear bottles so you can see the different pot-pourri textures. Use a pointed object to make small holes in the bottles to let the scent out. (These can be used to perfume drawers and make good presents for children to take home.)

▶ Try to make your own collection of pot-pourri using items from the garden, drying out plants, and using twigs and pieces of bark.

Conclusion

Being a reflective practitioner

Discovery bottles collections are as exciting and varied as your imagination and knowledge of child development will allow! Once you start using them and thinking about how children react and learn from these resources, you will see the range of possibilities. Whether you are in a nursery unit or class, a toddler or baby room, or if you are a nanny or a childminder in a home care situation, you and the children can enjoy making and using these bottles.

It is important to look, listen and note when children are making and playing with the bottles – observations are an important part of supporting and extending the learning process. How the child holds, looks at and reacts to the contents of the bottles, the gestures and speech they use and the other ideas triggered in your mind are all part of the process.